BLAZERS

HORSEPOWER

SUPERBIKES

by Mandy R. Marx

Reading Consultant:

Barbara J. Fox

Reading Specialist

North Carolina State University

Capstone *press*

Mankato, Minnesota

Blazers is published by Capstone Press,
151 Good Counsel Drive, P.O. Box 669, Mankato, Minnesota 56002.
www.capstonepress.com

Library of Congress Cataloging-in-Publication Data
Marx, Mandy R.
    Superbikes / by Mandy R. Marx; reading consultant, Barbara J. Fox.
    p. cm. — (Blazers—horsepower)
    Includes bibliographical references and index.
    ISBN 0-7368-4391-4 (hardcover)
    ISBN 0-7368-6172-6 (softcover)
    1. Superbikes—Juvenile literature. I. Fox, Barbara J. II. Title. III. Series:
Horsepower (Mankato, Minn.)
    TL440.15.M376 2006
    629.227'5—dc22   2005000559

Summary: Discusses superbikes, their main features, and how they are raced.

Credits
Jason Knudson, set designer; Patrick D. Dentinger, book designer;
    Kelly Garvin, photo researcher; Scott Thoms, photo editor

Photo Credits
Chicken Hawk Racing, 18
Getty Images Inc./AFP/Henny Ray Abrams, 24; Vincent Jannink, 25;
    Robert Cianflone, cover; Time Life Pictures/ Michael Stahlschmidt/Ssp., 11
Nelson, Brian, 5, 6, 7, 8, 9, 12, 13, 14–15, 17, 20–21, 23, 26, 28–29

1 2 3 4 5 6 10 09 08 07 06 05

TABLE OF CONTENTS

RACE DAY

Engines growl, and the smell of fuel fills the air. The biggest superbike race of the year has begun. It is the Daytona 200.

Mat Mladin leans into a turn on his number 1 Suzuki motorcycle. Suddenly, Mladin passes number 20 and pulls into the lead.

Puck

BLAZER FACT

Superbike racers wear shields on their knees called pucks.

Riders battle for second place
behind Mladin. The fans go wild.
Mladin has broken a record. He has
won his third Daytona 200.

DAYTONA
2004 SUPERBIKE CLASSIC
WINNER
DAYTONA INTERNATIONAL SPEEDWAY
DAYTONA
200
ROCKET
ROCKET
Team SUZUKI
TEAM YOSHIMURA
SUZUKI
RK
Racing Chain
NGK
SPARK PLUGS
MOTOREX
Oil of Switzerland
VP
Racing

SUPERBIKE DESIGN

Superbikes begin as regular street motorcycles. Mechanics work on them to get them ready for the racetrack.

Mechanics remove lights, mirrors, and turn signals. They change the engine to give it more power.

BLAZER FACT

Superbikes can go from 0 to 60 miles (0 to 97 kilometers) per hour in 3 seconds.

Fairing

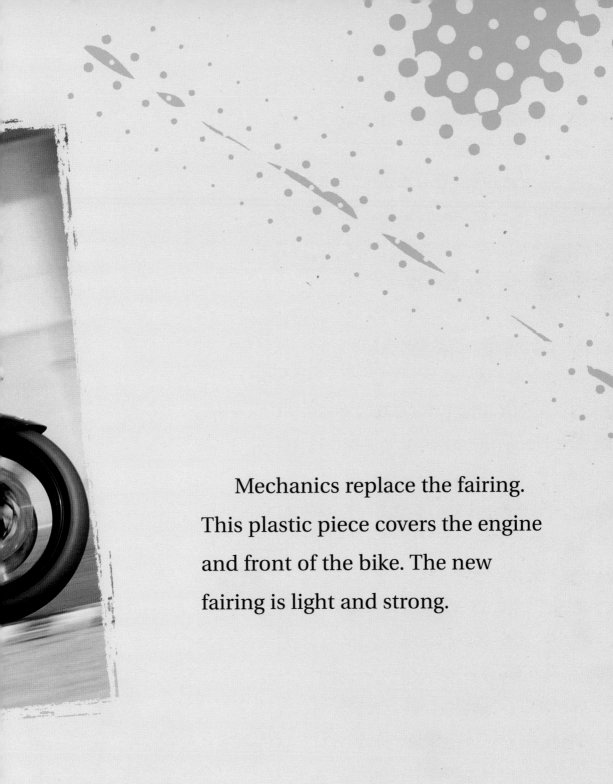

Mechanics replace the fairing. This plastic piece covers the engine and front of the bike. The new fairing is light and strong.

GRIPPING THE TRACK

Superbikes have special racing tires. They are made of soft, smooth rubber. This rubber grips the track.

Heater

In order to grip the track, tires must be hot. Racing teams use heaters to warm the tires before each race.

BLAZER FACT

Racing tires work best when heated to at least 212 degrees Fahrenheit (100 degrees Celsius).

Superbike Diagram

Puck

Tire

Handlebars

Fairing

Engine

THE RACING WORLD

Superbike racing thrills fans all over the world. Most races are 62 miles (100 kilometers) long. The top 30 finishers earn points.

In superbike racing, crashes can
be deadly. The American Motorcycle
Association (AMA) makes racers wear
helmets, leather suits, and back shields.

Superbikes do not have safety belts. If a crash occurs, it is safer for the rider not to be strapped to the bike.

Back shield

Helmet

BLAZER FACT

Mat Mladin has won five AMA
Superbike Championships.
He holds the record.

The AMA Superbike Championship
Series has 18 races. At the end of the
season, the racer with the most points
is the champion.

LEANING INTO A TURN!

GLOSSARY

durable (DUR-uh-buhl)—tough and lasting for a long time

fairing (FAIR-ing)—the covering over the engine and front end of a motorcycle

handlebars (HAN-duhl-barz)—the bars at the front of a superbike that are used for steering

mechanic (muh-KAN-ik)—someone who is skilled at operating or repairing machinery

puck (PUHK)—a protective shield worn on superbike racers' knees

shield (SHEELD)—a protective barrier

READ MORE

Graham, Ian. *Superbikes.* Chicago: Heinemann Library, 2003.

Ryder, Julian. *World Superbikes: The First Fifteen Years.* Newbury Park, Calif.: Haynes North America, 2002.

Sievert, Terri. *The World's Fastest Superbikes.* Mankato, Minn.: Capstone Press, 2002.

INTERNET SITES

FactHound offers a safe, fun way to find Internet sites related to this book. All of the sites on FactHound have been researched by our staff.

Here's how:

1. Visit *www.facthound.com*
2. Type in this special code **0736843914** for age-appropriate sites. Or, enter a search word related to this book for a more general search.
3. Click on the **Fetch It** button.

FactHound will fetch the best sites for you!

INDEX